# MORAINE

# MORAINE

Joanna Fuhrman

Hanging Loose Press
Brooklyn, New York

Published by Hanging Loose Press, 231 Wyckoff Street, Brooklyn, NY 11217-2208. All rights reserved. No part of this book may be reproduced without the publisher's written permission, except for brief quotations in reviews.

www.hangingloosepress.com

Printed in the United States of America
10 9 8 7 6 5 4 3 2 1

Hanging Loose thanks the Literature Program of New York State Council on the Arts for a grant in support of the publication of this book.

Cover art by the author
Cover design by Pamela Flint

Acknowledgments: The author gratefully acknowledges the editors of the following journals and websites, in which certain of these poems originally appeared: *The Brooklyn Rail, Conduit, Hanging Loose, The Hat, Lit, New American Writing, The New York Quarterly, The Saint Ann's Review, Spout, Titanic Operas, Turntable, Unpleasant Event Schedule*, and the *Verse Magazine Blog*, and the anthologies *Voices in the City* (Hanging Loose Press 2004) and *Experimental Theology* (The Seattle Research Project 2003).
Some of these poems also appeared in a chapbook called *Belladonna\* Moraine*, published by Belladonna Press. She would like to thank Erica Kaufman, and Rachel Levitsky for their work on that book. She would also like to thank the editors of Hanging Loose Press, and Marie Carter and Donna Brook for their work on this book. As always special thanks is owed to Jean-Paul Pecqueur, Noelle Kocot and David Shapiro, who were usually the first people to read these poems and helped in their development. Thanks is also owed to the Hall Center for the Arts and Education in Vermont where many of these poems were completed, and to Eileen Tabios and the 2005 Pleasurable Poetry Contest.

Library of Congress Cataloging-in-Publication Data available on request.

ISBN: 1-931236-53-4 (paperback)
ISBN: 1-931236-54-2 (cloth)

Produced at The Print Center, Inc. 225 Varick St., New York, NY 10014, a non-profit facility for literary and arts-related publications. (212) 206-8465

# Contents

~

~

~

~

*For Bob*

**Moraine (noun):**

A mound, ridge or ground covering of unsorted debris, deposited by the melting away of a glacier.

—*Geology Dictionary*

# ARCHITECTURE MORAINE

A woman builds a house out of birds' cries and cries
all the time within it. The man she had wanted says,

"I am looking for a woman who is crying, but can't
tell if anyone is crying inside that house's outer

crying. So she builds another house; this time, tears
for bricks, and cries as loud as she can within it.

Still he can't hear her because the house's
rectangular tears are too dazzlingly beautiful

to hear within. At this point, they both should be
laughing. The ceiling is neither of their mouths,

but full of teeth. The sky above: a chicken,
fresh out of a fake swamp, opening its eyes

and flashing its resplendent wings.


                    **


They called this coincidence
"summer" and continued
on their merry way.

She, like a man,
invisible when
opening a checkbook.

He, like a woman,
invisible when taking
off his clothes.

They both envied
text, only invisible
when someone

would claim it was
"poetry," like
a photograph,

only invisible
when said to be
"fact."

**

All walls lie.

Say somewhere an ocean is empty of leaves.

Say somewhere our dance is inside the roof's burnt-down need.

The red shoe calls out to be danced in.

The potato calls out to be held like a doll.

The house calls out to be as empty as poetry

And say, "yes, ma'am, I am empty as poetry."

And say, "yes, sir, I am the soft spot on the back of a scar."

Somewhere a harpsichord is weeping.

Somewhere someone can hear a harpsichord weeping.

Somewhere someone can hear a harpsichord weeping and tell us what
    the weeping is for.

A man holds a stethoscope to a woman's closed mouth.

A man holds a tongue out to another man's car.

This is just stereotype.

Those ideas:

a woman  a woman a woman a woman a woman a man.


          **


"Let's say all poems are a Band-Aid on the word.
Let's say a house is a poem that doesn't know it

once died. Then to be a woman is exactly like being
a man, but to be a man is unlike anything a woman

might possibly be."

> This was the song of the house on the brink of the room's
> smallest eye hat cursed two belted felt smile, two knocked up
> ideas, a prickly tremble inside a self made of nothing but noise,
> while room temperature barbecue butterfly shenanigans drip.

# Self-Portrait Moraine with Missing Tuba

Words rise up from me like lyrics to a song "Invalidate Me": a melody swallowed by an insect devoured by a whale…. Is that a beach ball inside the bottom of my forehead? Hours on end, I snorkel through thoughts, treading in and out, like shadows cast on hands. Corncobs shaped like ducks pile up outside the door of the job I lost.

Who bops along to these jammed resentments?

What's behind that particular gaggle of hipster noise?

I hold my breath until I hear my heart pounding in my chest. I hold my breath until I am a cave sliding into croon: a dark kind neural path where I can pretend I was once the nexus of multiple hatcheries, a pure stream of revenue flowing from these eyelids into dawn.

Here's where the starlit narrative comes in:

a child, age four, plays hide and seek alone behind a tree. A grown man tells me this to make me like him more. It works.

The radio eats the sound to hide the knife's new edge. The radio eats its voice to hide the talk of war. Women, I mean me, always flock to young hurt men. The sun controls us like a puppet's string. I write a note to burn the trash: "to poke out the light's fake eye?"

I hear some laughter coming from behind a door.

I write my name again. I write my name so large it is all I see. Then nothing happens. Nothing happens again.

A frog floats to the surface of a pond.

## Cento Moraine

Everything was withdrawn as far as possible:
shadows of boulders lengthened my back,

the little man inside the last individual brain,
like a long piece of raffish joy, passed through

a needle in ripples of applause, wholly
.abandoned so as to inhabit another world

more than this flecked thing: the cliffs
lodged to waves melded hingeless

flickered against the ceiling and set such
color there. I was thinking where are we all

going so small and gray? Frightened by the lack
of any real communication— forever futile,

rain-ravaged, root-ruined, the skeletons of umbrellas:
broken promises of casualness, life on the move,

a caravan of event making affection and all
the green winters wide awake. It is so sad.

It is so lonely feeling like a girl lest the thinking
appear as words: a consequence of somebody else's

unfathomable will. An involuntary gesture
to others not there? Baby riot's wet nighttime

tremor in the head before the being of ourselves
began majestically to engulf us, all the birds crying

as they wheel above; finally an emblem, the pivot
of a fresh being bedded in a choir of wings

like love being made between fire engines:
arrogant little waves knocking at the door—

worthless narcoleptic wombats. This is
the greatest possible drag! Wicked vistas!

The wolves mourn for our crime, green
and waking with weeds of the sea.

The largest motion—to, fro, up, down—
collapses to a steady but painful vibration,

frightful spaces down from all sides; it is
a wordless world without personality as if

it were a scene made up by the mind past sunset
in a corner of the beach: the usual gray rock.

# ROOM TEMPERATURE, A MORE PERSONAL MORAINE

Sitting on the Promenade not eating
the bagel next to me in a paper bag,
I try to relax, try to imagine myself shining
above myself: a star on a planetarium ceiling
in the middle of the day.  Wouldn't it be
better to write a more obviously honest poetry
like old Tu Fu, near death, dancing
and mocking his ragged cane,
his family sleeping inside? David says
only the young or really immature can write
exciting poetry. He keeps forgetting
I am over thirty now. Not as young
as he thinks, old enough to want
a more stable job, to try to start being
a little less blunt, more sure. I hope
the future of poetry will have nothing
to do with this desire for security.
Maybe then my white robes can just
burst into melody. I can stop being
trapped by the comforts of metaphor.
All I want is to slip out from under
this dumb brain, daily, if not hourly,
and into the electronic river I rename
by entering my idea of another,
kind of like the dream where I lose
my teeth and run around, proud
I am able to bleed.  How Jewish is that!
It should, *at least*, make up for dropping
Hebrew School, if not for dating only goys.
I think this would be a better poem
if it were really April, instead of November,
if my eyes had the darting charm of a preteen,
stuck in a doorway, full of impossibility.

I need to make a list of chores: send voided check
to job, write three more letters to look for work,
check out prices on laser printers.
My fingernails are cut all crooked.
A loud black and yellow sign screams:
"The Quiet Zone," and a gray-haired woman,
in a perfect pantsuit, jogs, pushing
an empty stroller over wet leaves.

# Approaching-Religious Moraine

*"without god there is no god"*
Joseph Ceravolo

A telephone is too anthropomorphic to be any use
as a religious icon. Likewise the ocean. Mama Mama.
Mood-enhancing field lines haul a radiant worn beginning
into the present we shun to approach ourselves:  mad needs

need wild honesty snow tuffs growing fractious throughout
the daisy patch past future falling thoughts where the not-
poem only only only only words and free of them or us
needs us less than we want to not want ice cream—(them?)

**

Song, I hate your demands! The thought of being lonely
is more and more shame. Cry in a public restroom then
read falling petals on the crashed eye's anemic opalescent shore.
"No island is a private language," they say. Slants of crocus

red pierces with a brazen loveliness like an early kind of Christmas
flickers for the Jews: chirpy, plucky, joy! Andy Warhol's brand
of hipster lipstick, reinvented from the grave for the lipless-wonders
of a New York we all love to hate? An idea for the new 1906.

**

Imagine it: the original first piece of buttered bread. I bet that tasted yum,
freed from memory's icky taint. I want that, that green green plate.
Factual Sunlight Madame! Two grains of sand in my hand: not in some
woman's pale hand first; they are nothing like these words I use to

order coffee or to attempt to pray. They are these geese, dividing the sky into a kind of nonabstract grid, or even like the blessed wallpaper designer growing inappropriately blissed out, giddy from drawing over and over again so many of the same same bird.

# Before Thinking Moraine

It was the *idea* of thinking
                    more than any particular thought
that drew me to the empty room.


            An awkward greenness hung over everything those days.


                    Two spiders alternated
                                    waves.


            **

All the water glasses line up.

This means I am an art student and a classmate is telling me about a forgotten ancient language in which the words for colors are named for rocks.

There are an infinite variety of rock types, so each shade of color has its own distinct name: indisputable, known, clear.

Misunderstanding can never occur because each color word meaning is exact.

Hearing this story, I feel an almost religious rush: my mind contracts and expands.

Later, the other student finds the original genera of rocks and carves them into a series of identically shaped roses. Under each flower, she makes a sign with a translation of its forgotten name.

I try to take the markers down.

**

I can't hear the edges slipping,

can't *say* where the ocean

might end and a filled thimble begin.

If there is a "meaning" in the area,

I feel oddly despondent as if only *I* should understand

the subtext of each seltzer bubble in the glass.

True glory?
Damn sunrise—

# Post-Suburban Moraine

All along I knew the razzmatazz beauty was said to conjure
was just a weary catalogue, a thermometer designed to make us
sick, a pox dividing a house already split and licked. I'd vow
"enough!" until I could no longer speak. I'd start a list: 1) shred
TV; 2) flip another synchronized swimmer against the carpeted wall.
 "Guard yourself too much and appliances become the most treasured
relics in the world," I'd warn my dolls, ingrate in their holy stupor,
        drunk,
staring at the floor (just because they could?). Why didn't they ever
notice the IQ kiosk laughing at us, slapping its sides like a comic book cop.
Didn't they understand there is no human zoo? Mild evenings crush the sky
so often nuclei become a substitute for time, but still, I am "myself":
a woman who waits in line to buy a toothbrush, the daughter of the
        letter "a",
a box of condoms melting in the sun. All day, I listen for the child crying
at a birthday party while her parents divorce themselves from the film's
script, my room ovulating above the sea, above the bar where failed
football players neck in the corner where every song the jukebox plays
is a link to a roller rink circa 1983, where streamers drape around the
        indoor
fire-hydrant, mumbling, "yeah, yeah, yeah" and the wet unread chapter
of the book on gerunds, and why we shouldn't use them, keeps falling apart,
scattering so we can no longer see our reflection in the bare floor's
        brazen austerity.
"Pliant whispers are just a substitute for real (i.e. direct) speech," they
        want us
to believe,  their muzak quickening in every fake vein, an alternate arm
        spilling out
like OJ rushing into a sunlit-data-filled hole? One of us might as well be
a turnip.
One of us might as well be cradling a gun named "Sweet Lee Ann".
        Might as well
be jumping off a one-foot cliff to another cliff below. Don't you understand,

I just want to be corrected: punched to the south. Too honest to be a
good healer,
I try. I try to understand the latent compassion in all dull knives. Peach
pits sob in private.
Centipedes measure the coordinates of the evening's curved and broken
handle.
Blisters bloom like mushroom clouds over our era's nostalgic diorama of
tragic kitsch, while the tax returns fight back: brave, groovy, and strong
against the strident
ukulele, against the hot and blistered moped, against the moping
Victorian ideal.
"There is no such thing as a broken bridge or a rough code," a billboard
announces.
Except in words? These. These words. Another syllabic mutation called
meaning.
Another carpe diet soda, my bro. A rude wind that only blows us twig to
fig. Just
beginning, middle and end. Another hummingbird not humming.
Another cat envying
the computerized version of its stroll. Xerox the copies of your eyelids
while you are
still allowed. "Remember the mandolin playing in the dark before the
rivaling lost
voice box tried to rob zero of its loss?" Pretend you are that note. Pretend
the moon
is just a punctured hole in the night sky. Pretend you are the screw in
the fraught
diving board. Another avocado rolls. Another penny loses value.
Another cactus
pricks the empty space inside an atom. I have been writing the same
sentence all my life
with different words. I have tried to be a good friend, but all those
actions kept getting
in the way of my words. All of the pets in the pet store escape from their
cages
when I close my eyes. The man my therapist claims I am in love with
opens and

closes a cab door in the rain near a bowling alley in Eastern Mass. My
        therapist
is wrong, what I felt was never love, just another trope, a temporary
        resting place
for unfettered desire like a clear blue tube filled and refilled with gushing
        colored water
until it moves or breaks. The driver is already in another state, off duty,
        eating
scrambled eggs in a diner where he thinks he has a crush on the thin
        blond waitress
with the smile, pouring coffee into his not yet empty cup because cab
        drivers in poems
always have crushes on such waitresses, and besides the scar he imagines
        on her perfect hip
is identical to his own, and this is one of the writer's  (I guess, my)
        favorite romantic
myths. The pets return to their cages when we open our eyes. The penis
        in my dream
dangles by a purple teddy bear. My friends will make fun of me because
        there
are so many stuffed animals in my poems.  The lights return to their
        sockets
when we screw them back in. The flowers by the window turn to silk
        when we take
their picture. The scent of a hamburger grilling is shaped like a supermodel
if we inhale the right combination of drugs. The words in the book turn
        to dance steps
when riding in a moving car. The sun in the painting burns our clothes off
when we are already naked. Music is a reason for rooms.

# Pulp Novel Viewed through a Thingamabob Moraine

He was two separate baby boys dressed in the frills of a single pineapple, so he had to wear his grown-up sadness pasted to the outside of another's face. The woman in the bleachers loved this and tied a phone cord around his neck as a reward.

Taking the metaphors out of sex would be a challenge, they agreed, not easily accomplished in the time they had allotted to the task.

So long, magnificent marigolds, fresh mornings in Hanoi, fly swatters! "Sacrifice" would be the requisite catchword for their newly anointed endeavor; a fuzzy rat-shaped pencil top, their only other pal.

# You Should Have Been There for the Hangover! Moraine

I was all geeked out
in my "Poetry Rules!" T-shirt
and kneepads when the rain
washed away my attempt
at a rondeau. Frank O'Hara,
wethaired and giddy, jumped off
the coffee mug to grab me
by the anklet and haul my ass
to the living museum where
people stay still and action
paintings roam, nipping you
with their claws if you only stand
far from the surface or describe
them with too many
Latinate terms. It's all
Lite Brites and pick-up
sticks in the spondee nightclub
from then on, the penis
on Walt Whitman digitally
enhanced, Muriel Rukeyser
holding her oar above the peaks
of puny waves, Nicanor Parra
ripping out the pages that are
more boring than the blank,
and Andre Breton with a wet
Sit-and-Slide and a purple whip,
bossing everyone about, while
Álvaro de Campos, Ricardo Reis,
and Alberto Caerico play
rock, paper, scissors to determine
the final resting place of
Fernando Pessoa's dentures

which keep chattering under
the glitter balls, and singing
ballads about Lorca's pet hen
who has escaped the "I'm-feeling-
ill-at-ease-in-my-suburban-
living-room-sonnet-poultry -
butcher" and is now shaking
out his kaleidoscopic glass
and fire feathers, and squawking
obscene-duende limericks about
baseball and bubble gum and
florescent hydroponic ballet.

# SERIOUS MORAINE

A joke and a tear wrap their eyes in blindfolds and step on the scale before it breaks. A joke and a tear put ice cubes on their tongues and step into the ocean before it turns to steak. If you want to know the difference between them, make mad mad love to one while your toe is hunting for creamsicles in the clammy-ham wilds of the other.

**

The smallest clown in the world writes an autobiography, starring a tear and a joke. Anyone who reads it is punched in the face and brought to the cute balloon guy at the mall. He is as good in bed as a joke. "Friends", he says, "we are as multiple as we are dumb. The aliens who visit us in our dreams are actually pet rocks and can go nowhere except a movie theater."

**

I wanted to write that "a joke and a tear polkaed on the deck of a polka-dotted cruise ship," but my pen was less versatile than my brain. It poked out my eyeballs and threw them in the gumball machine that was already full of other people's eyeballs. How humiliating! To be upside down in what was once a sea of chewable bubbles? To roll perhaps to gleam!

**

A joke and a tear take over the devastated city and turn all the museums into souvenir mausoleums. A joke and tear slither into the same discarded snakeskin. They broadcast their pronouncements by slipping a pillowcase over their heads and singing their own words to the theme from *All in the Family*. "Joke + Tear Best Friends 4-eva'," a girl takes down in pink ink.

# NOT REALLY MEDIAL, A MORAINE?

I don't need to touch that particular anthropomorphic
cantaloupe to imagine the young man's mind, tender

as a number in a poem about roofing. With him,
I am that girl in droopy pigtails, pretending to drown

in her best friend's swimming pool, bubbles
floating to the surface like a color-saturated

cartoon where no one can die or bleed.
Who says a minor petal is any less devastating

than a major punch? Can't they see
the drama in feeling things from the outside in:

a clear glass owl's eye splitting light
into a multiplex of shreds.
                              Listen—          the piano's

        divertimento:
a spider crawling my leg.

My nose pressed up against the glass.
        The buffalo's heroic connotations

close to obscene. A red sweater too big
                    to *not* sink in.

Oh dear Monster-Truck Derby of the Soul!
                        Lasso somethin' up,
                                    you brute!
I'm sick of these
            incipient bits.

## NIGHTTIME MORAINE

To fall into the *here* of it—as if the workers sleeping
in the skyscraper don't mind the rain banging against
the windows and I am not the car being driven under
the river. A voice in my ear whispers: *bend your head
down and close your eyes, pretend your hands are
slipping to the bottom of the horse's mane.*
                        No fear is here:
the filmstrip of a man holding a woman's foot whose head
is hidden by a lion's mask is projected on the inside
of my feather pillow.
        Who would have thought that any image
would be universal enough to span the gap between the voice
booming over the lake's orange triangle and that other origin—
the so called "emptiness" where people meet and forget
each other, a dark car mirror in the middle of a blackout
or a sparrow's nest before a child is old enough to name it.

**

While Shirley Temple warbles "Good Ship Lollipop"
(—higher than usual? ) I am, for the moment, brushing her wet curls
in the pool and also watching myself (and her) on a screen. This isn't
the film that made the song famous, but I've witnessed this moment
        before—
seen it replayed many times on television screens in small hotel rooms.
Shirley murmurs, "I want to swim to find the soul emanating
from the swimming pool light"

and

"we will one day exit the side where fish devour
their own shadow."

**

A bed is shifting in the night. A core is removed from a white apple. A spotlight falls in my eyes. A puppeteer, my friend's new boyfriend, is in the living room, showing us his lovely bare hand, still on the coffee table.

His finger's lack of movement is almost pornographic.
Glorious. Supine.

**

There is—at any one moment—

an abundance of regions where we are not disgusted
by our fingers stained yellow from the theater's popcorn,
or where the wheels in grainy old movies don't fracture
into kaleidoscopic critiques of our desire to move.

**

A couple I have never met is in love,
and I am *supposed* to feel happy for them.

Shirley Temple's voice falls from the trees like a net.

Someone unseen and unknown forces us to board a small plane.

The type of plane you enter by pullout stairs.

It makes me feel like a head of state or the head of state's wife.

There is something surprising and erotic about imagining myself framed by the paparazzo's flash, but there is no one watching.

It is raining and my ticket is blank.

## Theater Moraine

Tonight every play in this city
is the same damn play:

      the college girl discovers
      she's only a bitch
      because she wants to be loved,
      the mother discovers
      she's only a jerk because
      her father died young.

But what is the role of the aquarium, stage right,

      what of the bare knee of the unkissed
      data specialist, audience rear?

    **

A poem and a play
meet in the middle
of the night disguised
as bats. Insects dressed
as pirates sing too softly
for either to hear. It is
New Year's on the horizon
so they huddle under
an azalea in the blue
tangerine of a milked
blink.

    **

Dramaturge:
We will ask the playwright to make it clear.

Director:
We will ask the actor to make it real.

    Actor:
    I was a child in white boots in a white house.

    Actor:
    I was a teenage egghead counting pigeons in a truck in suburbia.

    Spotlight:
    We were made to flummox and fail.

    Actor:
    My mother drank instead of playing gin.

    Actor:
    I was left alone to till the fields.

# Basement Office Moraine

Telephone operators are more than just shamanic;
a storm of swapping cords, they are possessed
and hear nothing but their own frenetic soundtrack,
crashing before wires dive and disappear.

Being one of them is like riding a bicycle no
hands down an underwater rake, the ceiling
above: a reversible mirror, splattered with image
and racing to the stairs' waterfall. Like few others,

they understand the sadness of being a mere
medium, the loss paint feels when it leaves
the tube and how every word thrown into use
longs for the sweet womb of a closed dictionary.

\*\*

For many years, I walked in slippers while the jailer knitted a key to slip
around my neck. All of the exit signs were replaced with a picture of
Snoopy hanging off a cliff. I was happy enough. I was a million congruent
verbs hanging from a roof: a little red ball in a pack of jacks, hopping
about in a hotel bathroom. If I wanted to make love, I could throw my
mind and the monitor out separate windows and they'd land in the same
cellophane ocean below.

\*\*

I said: "To follow an operator is to abandon love."

He said: "A hallway flies open inside you."

I said: "I am nothing, but a pen and its thin dark cousin."

He said: "Another hallway is a bird's long neck."

I said : "My eyes are closed."

He said : "I can see a tongue in an open mirror."

I said: "I can see a tractor's jaw."

He said: "Our office sanctuary needs no windows. "

I said: "Dark tubes poke out of that tilted wall."

## Brooklyn Efficiency Apartment Moraine

The television kept flying under my Keds.

First it was a rainbow-bass-striped jump rope, then a muted buzzing. "Are you my little pet god?" I asked the sleeping vacuum cleaner, its eyes moldable like stiff beaten egg whites. "Will you be my Jiminy Cricket?" I queried the dust bunny as it waltzed toward a lounging slant of light, toward the watch submerged in a tumbler of gin, toward the moon with its nose ring transmitting messages.... A light was on and then it was off.

I felt proud to walk across dark wet Sixth Avenue, humming to myself.

# Cento Moraine #2

1)

My laughter is the fire of the eye of the sky.
Write that down. The impossible disembodied roar!
An overstatement? Beautiful half-hour of being
a mere woman? A wisp of girl trapped in a golden halo
foreheads wrinkled with injunctions like a shell
surrendered to evening sands? Shame encore there:

music, the mosaic of the air along tarred rooftops
stretching invisibly into the future so as to reappear
in our present, riveted to the unrealizable.  All fire afire
with thunderous noise & dreadful shakings, rocking
to & fro. Bards freezing, naked, up to the neck in water,
time before and time after, down among the lost

people like Dante immersed in the depths,
reforming a definition backward and outward so close
to nonsense that the mind shuttles beneath shade,
sleep flowering casually over the windows all
fogged with breath, a narrow moment narrowly
cemented, now dark—now glittering—now reflecting

gloom.  I miss your absence as I miss my own.
The peopled and the unpeopled: they are the lost case.
Am I wrong? I used to imagine you were a fine two-
headed animal, rigorously going from field to field,
obedient to the strong creative power of human passion,
resurrection music,      silence    and surf.

2)

There is no longer any use in harping on.
Something weirdly architectural between one thought
and the next is what they wanted. It is a lost road into
the air, a black line beside a white line a year a year
a year to another. Look through these binoculars & you
will see one thousand small-town New England greens:

a state thick as a fist or a blunt instrument.
The voice that used to call you home has gone off
in the wind. I think my eyes are empty.
The army needs parts and the parts need a job to do.
Welcome television to this rug-ruined room.
To look for meaning is as foolish as to find it.

The sickness of this age is flesh: static scene after
static scene. The sun beats lightning on the waves.
Bats come in place of swallows, airliners passing
over them at the dead of Midwest midnight.
Everyone young going down the long slide, clean
and unbroken lines of concrete. There's a billion

starry nights out there. When the night comes
small fires go out.  Disordered speech coiled within
cobalt miles of sky,  the resonance of every image
I had tried to cut from my brain flattened
to the pavement far below. Two, of course,
there are two.

# Swing Set Moraine

*(for Bob Kerr)*

"*Ah ha*," "we are now fast approaching    the version of ourselves
we attempt to simulate through art,"

                    that great sequin we can pretend is home,
                    a thousand feathers floating
in a seasick vacuum ruffling our brains,  oh our adult
doubles,     hanging    in subcommerce's dazzling stream.
                    Who said? Who said, "There can be
                    no ringing in a deaf bird's ear?"


Those people! People.
                    They don't know. No,
they *don't* know.

                    How it feels.


          **


Our relatives were surprised that writers could
swing. They had seen the *New Yorker* film version
and that wasn't included. I tried to explain, "it's
like this only in Brooklyn, Queens or in the
Poconos. Everywhere else the literati have to
travel in stubby lifeboats called iambic narratives
and write essays about the dangers of seeing the
world through more than one eyelid. Everywhere
else the readers are chained to the rail…."


              **

You knew exactly how and when to put an end to
        the excess of my provincial ranting, so
                you kissed me
      on my lips by touching my elbow.
While we were making love, your play was produced in fifty-four languages
        in all kinds of eras,
         they memorized your lines all over
         the playground and way past the river....

Everywhere they belted out your made-up slang.
           Even in the Midwest.
Even the sad parts:
the stage directions.

# MORAINE FOR BOB

You were never a man
in the television sense of the word.

I was never a wild Slinky
in the sex-club sense of a toy.

You were never a tobacco store
in the Modernist sense of a trope.

I was never a snowdrop
in the candy store sense of a treat.

You were never Day-glo
in the fashionista sense of a scarf.

I was never *withyouallthetime*
in the username sense of a self.

You were never a strumpet
in the toothache sense of an insult.

I was never a tooting horn
in the childhood sense of a game.

You were never a hole-in-my-heart
in the country singer sense of a vista.

I was never a paper doll
in the pyromaniac sense of a pal.

You were never a parenthesis
in the phony secret sense of a sign.

I was never red lipstick
in the pulp novel sense of a threat.

You were never a word
in the mystic sense of an obstacle.

I was never a shaking castanet
in the midnight sense of a song.

# Brooklyn Efficiency Apartment Moraine #2

You drove your toy car into the tub so I would dive for it, holding my breath. Your cock turned somersaults in the mirror's amphitheater until that game turned into what I was young enough to believe was a new form of symphonic notation: a canary's brainwaves flowing through the pages of magazines.

We were both conscious of a certain same feeling. It wasn't like being awkward in the locker or at the doctor's.

The room might have been wearing a trench coat. There was a knocking from beneath a knee.

# PINCHED KITCHEN PARTIAL-MORAINE, A LULLABY

nubby stars
mock us

when they
revolve

no oil
hot enough

to splash
them back

into their
corset

so I am
again

just voice,
and you

again just
ear, covered

and numb
like the memory

of a faucet's
splattered

kiss

# Mellow Pad Moraine

(for B)


All afternoon I feel faint, gulp diet ginger ale,
sweep the living room, hide the condom wrappers
under the yellow pillow instead of walking to the trash.
"Drinking water is a better cure for dizziness
than lovemaking, but harder to start." This is why
I am a poet and not a data entry specialist and why
the sun hits the Carmen Miranda shaped salt and pepper
shakers only in the dream called "Sunday." What good
is anxiety anyway except as fuel for mass hand-holding
marathons, blitzed-holiday-shaggy dancing by the sink.


**


I am in love with you, but in the dream called "apple"
I have no memory of who you are, or where. The room
loses a wall, and so the clear wall behind it takes its place.
A basement with a fake wood-paneled wet bar is revealed,
shiny and multifaceted as a mask. Men in Fifties swim
trunks pour tiki drinks into their shorts, and I am so happy
the empty shape of a memory beside me splits in two,
each part a mirror for the other until one shifts, the other blinks.
The music from yesterday is a rowboat on the mouth
of a sink. Somewhere a slanted room is already wrecked.


**


"The sky is pink as colored lemonade. Pink as a toenail
in the first color photograph of a baby's foot," I babble on.
"I am too exhausted to fall asleep tonight, so let's just talk."

The cat, she purrs. She elevates her ass so you will stroke it
with a rubber brush. We gush about our summer goals:
a train trip to the beach, a visit to your friend in Montreal
who took my favorite snapshot of you, legs akimbo, eyes
bulging, in a parody hippy-boogie. "You know, I still
have yet to see you do that dance for real!" You roll your eyes.
My thumb and finger creep your covered arm.

# BROOKLYN EFFICIENCY APARTMENT MORAINE #3

First I had the wrong brain and the right face. Then, the right face and the wrong brain. I hid my mouth in my pencil dispenser and slid under the bed. This was the year of the fraudulent key ring, sliding the length of the tape roll's teeth. I couldn't tell a wisecrack from a crack in an ass, couldn't tell my boyfriend's hand from the hand of a clock. Who knew that five chickens in an oven were worth none in a tree? I swam into the toilet bowl's mouth in a mile wide bra, dousing the river's trickle with ink from a once-burnt check.

## Spinal Moraine

My friend burned off his arms and legs
so he'd have something to remember
as he floated in his serpentine canoe.
Later that night, the sun was an equal
sign drawn by a finger in air, erased
by a headless vacuum tube.
*Tweet tweet paddlehoney suckle*
*ditti-o*, he would sing to a miniature
tape recorder stapled to his shirt.
His pain became a glorious relief,
an opalescent halo burning shadows
into light to make them shine.
           "This is not a dream," yelled
the red lingerie following him on a raft
down the tightest river's curve.
           "This is not a linguistic ornament,"
read the fine print, the expression on his face
shifting into marginal procedural drift.

*friend,*

*if you want to dress up as a sailor, you must first fight the ocean its handkerchief guile. if you want to dress up as a bride, you must first use your veil as a weapon to shield the moon from prurient intent.*

*i know you are not the sort to question the validity of a dear friend's order; you have spent a dozen childhoods laid out on white lace day beds, memorizing the plots of sexless soap operas, waiting for the evening's blunt return.*

We were born
two different kinds
of Fridays. I was once
as sad as a broken oar.
You were once

the millionaire
of the burning air.
     Our talk had
been as luminous as
the cut-glass rose, now
it's that baby's drool,
the tentative
bite.

# Partial Escapist Moraine

*(For Noelle)*

Let's pretend we're on a trip.
Rip out the moldy sky,
package our emotions into even intervals
so the jury will have no doubt about our business
acumen. No need to send another secret greeting
to the corporate Santa or an industrial fruitcake
to the temp agency. Don't worry about our poetry lessons.
They'll be kept private; our pronouncements
wrapped in the silk of the president's stolen panties, a pack
of intellectual wolves steering the boat
through the afternoon's amusement ride, your husband,
that sweet animal, no longer trapped under death's shield.

You, no longer sad.


**

I am sorry I can't help you today.
I should be ashamed. You know
I pray to my atheist god to make me ashamed, to be a train
to take you away, a joy train,
unashamed, light
as the train
that separates the sun's cells
as they gleam
the lights in your name more awake
than this death conglomerate was ever asleep.

# THEATER MORAINE #2

Inside a photo booth by a skating rink in a rundown Texas mall, the actress meets the woman her favorite role was based on and pretends to forgive her death.

Actor A:
The photo booth is transformed into a hospital.

Actor B:
The stretcher is light as a ghost.

Spotlight:
These blocks are the craggy steps to the great wall.

> *not theater. not*
> *thunder. not.*
>
> *inside an apple.*
> *not an ocean*
>
> *swallowing. not*
> *direct. not*
>
> *a grave. not*
> *air.*

It is raining inside the hardhat floating above their borrowed bodies.

It is snowing inside the mitten clamped to the actress' sleeve.

Child A:
What's behind the magic?

Child B:
Casters.

# Alchemy Moraine with Extra Microchip

We unpacked what
I thought was mystery
and found a horse
straddling a precipice.
I said, "take off your
plywood wings and
I will ride you to
the center of a digit."
I could see my own
brain glue bubbling
on the plastic flowers.
In the orange kitchen,
the replicas of my heart's
tubes hung, while my
favorite rock star
prayed to the
luminary computer.

\*\*

I was angry at that horse. I was angry *as* that horse. The horse became
another name for anger. Its huge white teeth: a substitute. The mirrors of
its eyes: my only way to see.

\*\*

Have you
ever felt this

small
as small as
my small
breasts,
your only
origami
frog folded
from a
postcard
of false
tears?

# METROPOLIS MORAINE

When they shut
our city down,
I was dreaming
of an identical one.
The moonlight twisted
like a clarinet solo
or a young skater's
first televised
double lutz.
My lover at the time
was living in a different
identical city and
emailing photographs
of our friends'
doppelgangers
to my account.
In a note to him,
I questioned
the veracity of time,
arguing it was possible
to slow it down,
to exist in a moment
together without
the previous and subsequent
crowding it out.

**

I could feel my organs growling a melody in their closet,

an indignant note in the margins of a dictionary.

In a letter I read that I should tie my hands behind my back and pray to the god of lost microbes.

The frog's blood in my ice cube flowed perpendicular to the airplane path.

This would be the "yellow period" in what would become known as "my life," followed by the "willow stage," and the great "clog era,"

all built to be forgotten.

\*\*

*Did you miss watching your shadow eat his apple under the visages of wild ostriches?*

*Could you open your mouth without revealing your tongue?*

*Did you sleep with your copy of* The Best Bad Poets *as a weapon under your neck?*

The questions continued
like a rainstorm in a movie
filmed in what used
to be a factory.
      The parrot I tied to
      my wrist refused
      to engage so I was left
      opening fortune cookies
      in the moonlight alone.

            *How long could the diary of the wandering comma*
            *continue without wanting a break?*

            *Did you purposely forget to name*
            *the city you bore?*

# SCHOOL DAYS LOST SONG MORAINE

*All I wanted was*
*to whisper to that girl*
          *"love is just a color*
*you wear on*
          *your lips," and*
*"you need to*
          *scoop out those tears*
*with a spoon,"*


\*\*


A first-grader in a conflict resolution workshop says to the other kids in her mime group, "I am a sponge in a sink." But the boy in her group is intent on being a basketball player. He crouches down and pretends to dribble a ball. The workshop leader complains that they are not IN-TER-ACT-ING with each other; they should think of a place all of them could be in *together* and act *that* out. The girl says, "All I've ever wanted is to be a sponge in a sink." Another girl says, "I like being a sponge in a sink too." Soon the girls are all chanting. "I am a sponge, a sponge in a sink."

But the boy ignores them. He dribbles his imaginary ball.


\*\*


*Too many rivers under*
*the same broke-down subway line.*
*Too many flower petals*
*drowning in an open sink.*
*Polished stem-gunk. Spilt*

*soy beverage. The smell*
*of an old margarine tub*
*on a thumb in the sun*
*on the last day of May.*

**

The teacher asks the students to think of something they could all do together. "Well," the girl says to her teacher, "We can all be in a kitchen, and I can be a sponge in a sink, and he can be a basketball player."

"Wouldn't his playing cause the dishes to break?" the teacher asks.

"No," the three-foot girl explains, "he will be a basketball player not playing ball."

# BAYONET MORAINE

I drove an ambulance across
my mother's face, then across
the face of every other ruined city,
petals scattered on hapless travelers
so when the rotunda finally fell,
the transaction transformed me—
I became a melody behind closed
eyes; my vehicle became my dick,
a joke of a sword, the war releasing
a thousand others' blood inside my own,
doves dying in smoke, a new
shade of red, a day lit up inside me
like a nightingale or a triple
honeymoon before a botched birth.

**

Other women are crying.
Other women are always

crying. I am not a mother
so I have no right to cry.

The male poets write
of the mothers crying.

I know. I was a male
poet once. I wrote

of my own mother
crying. She was

crying for a son
who was not me.

**

First I was a man.
I shot an apple off the head of a mermaid.

Then I was a woman.
I danced in the eye of a congressman's wife.

Then I was a man again.
The monorail twisted through the hydra.

Then I was a woman again.
My breasts: life preservers for opposing armies.

**

Oh, sunny apparition,
be my bourbon and my
marijuana, sweet shadow
in the marrow. What faith
is there in sycamore
or fire?

# CHILDREN'S SONG MORAINE

Meet the rattle man, the sun's best friend,
who sleeps in the midst of crowds and crowded
highways, and lugs elephant bells to the purple
river and hypnotizes the soldiers as he shimmies
on the river bank in his voluminous cravat,
and deserts the pudding angel through dry
grasses and dirty ditches, and embraces a turgid

disgust for sidewalk death. Oh rattle man,
he wants not, no, he wants no part in the pallor,
that bloody clearing, the orange button
decorated with bodies and bone roses.
Rattle man, he knows war is not the opposite
of a sunrise, he can separate the eyelid
from the eye, can open the can of the sky

into a thousand other fleeting possibilities
each as fragrant as a sweating petunia. Yeah,
the rattle man knows there is no need
to swim into a collective dream of glory,
knows the palatial floating resting home
of the clouds will always be open to him,
separate from his love of people and the real.

Does this mean he can balance a tiger in the eye
of a needle, that he can sew his name into the sky's
ruffles? He is perhaps, like many folks, open
to considering this option. He wears a crown
on his afro soldered with the finest lead.
He knows his way around a bottle of magnesium
and has swallowed his identity so many times

in so many varied incarnations he can open

his tongue to the sky and not feel it growing
like a lit wand inside his mouth .The rattle man
is not a liar, one trapped by a literal idea of truth.
He is not a master of speech fluctuation rendering
devices or qualified semantic iconic variations.
He is not an expert in incarceration techniques.

The rattle man is a friend to the earth, the air
and the sea. He is a hero to the electronic seals
who watch over us when we dream about the paddleboat
voyages through silver sewers. He is a mentor to all
the butterflies in the world, especially those born
in butterfly museums by ancient highways in forgotten
suburbs. He is with us when we are not even with ourselves.

He is a mensch times ten. He is a key on a string, struck
by the future's lightning. He is a jolly grandfather and
a sucked thumb. He is the inside of a ball of yarn,
the moss on an apple rolling down a mountain of beans.
He is a bullhorn to those who refuse to accept the inevitability
of battle. He is the mother of space and the father of breath.
He is the talk show therapist of the singing frogs.

# SELF-PORTRAIT AS INFANT MORAINE

I was born on the tracks during a railroad strike, and then again on a down pillow in the palace of Versailles. My father brushed my scars with vinegar to keep flies from my corpse. My mother shined my silver rattle so I could see reflections of my servants from my crib.

In both lives, I wanted milk, a lullaby, some eyes I might recognize among the lurking shapes.

**

When the video camera approached,
the geese in the sky flew backward.

When the strike was quashed,
my mother shook her guitar

and yelled at the printing press
to erase the number of workers dead.

My father was high on the mountain
building a stronghold out of birds' wings.

My mother was the sound
of a falling slipper.

**

To understand the inside of a baby, hold her up to the light.

You can watch her dream about a doll-in-a-basket floating
under a bridge in the city where she was born.

If she is a rich baby, dollar signs will float around her liver.

If she is a poor baby, mockingbirds will poke apart her lungs.

If she is somewhat in between, her insides will be as pristine as a nice hotel.

Do not dab the baby with butter.

Do not put the baby on the television set.

Even if you refer to her as Marty,

she will not be able to predict the weather.


                    **


In the painting of me, a violin imitates the squawk of a crow.

I am wearing a bonnet and sobbing, and then I am wearing
a potato sack and staring straight ahead.

In the recording of my voice, one can hear a lady mouse nibbling
on an ear-shaped soap, she is singing labor ditties and swinging
from the ropes of a velvet curtain.

I have heard the grown-ups murmuring that she had always been lousy
at following orders,

that her name in Esperanto means "delicate thug."

# FOUNTAIN MORAINE

I wear an advertisement for my best self
across my chest, a gold tuba wails against
the whimwham of the moon, a reunited table
and chair pull out a strand of hair, fresh
as the string of a butterfly. Glorious cinemas
entertain the prefight roosters, fragrant leaves
hiding the smell of humbugging elixirs, blossoming
trash cans trashing the piazza, a spirit of a new
ideal flying beyond our heads, the yearning
parade growing rudimentary leaves, heliotropic,
corporeal, sideways as a love letter or the after-
effects of a fistfight in a movie, open loonytoon
automatic time/space charade as if a photograph
of a naked gun is more opaque than the waning
fire truck growling through the freed slave district.

**

It is not a sign (a mark of dissolve) but a nowhere.

*Our* nowhere. Against stillness and chaos.

The nowhere of a photograph of a star.

The quiet of a shoelace.  The beginning of an old stillness.

Not unlike a paper tear glued to a cheek.

Not unlike a beach

where we sit and imagine ourselves

as ourselves. Not unlike a newspaper

swallowed by a pink-tinted whale.

No. Yes. No. The crackling.

The crackling of serious stars.


**

I sobbed and was unsold, or so I claimed.
The reasons were fraught with do-little bells,
isolated frequencies, benign widgets and monthly
visits to the ontology doctor who would watch me
in my sleep, and whisper the details of crumpled
post-it notes in my ear.
       There was an intimacy to this,
       his warnings balanced beside
       my blushing cheek, the promise
       of shared truth rubbed
       on my chest, thick as oil.